EGBEGUN FESTIVAL…

& its Political Economy

ANTHONY NWEKE

DEDICATION & ACKNOWLEDGEMENT

This book is dedicated to Professor Samson O. Olaitan, and all the inhabitants of No. 5 Mbanefo Street, UNN, Nsukka campus, at the time of this research. You all know yourselves… And to everyone who helped make this book possible, you are Awesome. Thank You for everything.

CONTENTS

CHAPTER ONE

INTRODUCTION

Yorubaland's renewed and invigorating attention to cultural events and tradition is increasingly visible in the performance of popular local and national festivals. As is common in traditional societies, membership in select groups is more often than not ascribed. Traditional festivals in Nigeria generally go to project the various aspects of the people's artistic and cultural heritage. Individuals become members of a group that performs the esoteric rituals of festivals by virtue of kinship ties, rank, office or other predetermined factors. They put on the festivals, a religious stamp that in the final analysis they are intended to bear.1

However, the roles of those responsible for dictating the nature of these festive events are also evolving in response to the country's economic agenda. Using the Egbegun Festival of Omuooke Ekiti in historical perspective, this work examines the role of festivals in the political economy of Yorubaland. In many ways traditional festivals are the past made present, which as historical constructs, may legitimate actions of the present.2

Festivals such as the Egbegun Festival of Omuooke Ekiti, no doubt, are now the arena in which many issues within Yorubaland's political economy are actively played out. The Egbegun Festival of Omuooke Ekiti is the cultural festival that contributes to the preservation of the age-long oral tradition of Omuooke people. It is one of the most cherished and highly valued festivals in the town and it involves graduations and initiations of one grade to another. The Egbegun Festival is one of the festivals in Yorubaland that follow a set liturgical pattern and this must be correctly carried out if the festival is to retain its efficacy. J. K. Parratt in his view, posited that the religious heritage of Ife is rich indeed and with Ife being the age-long spiritual home of the Yoruba, this heritage is a valuable source of information both about the history and the traditional religion of the Yoruba people.3

The historical origin of the Egbegun Festival of Omuooke Ekiti draws its links from Ife and this will be discussed in this study. As it has been stated, traditional festivals in Nigeria generally and specifically among the Yoruba, go to project the various aspects of the people's artistic and cultural heritages. The Egbegun Festival of Omuooke Ekiti, aside from its age-long preservation of history, is one that is cherished and highly valued by the Omuooke community. However, very little is known about the festival outside the community. So much work has been written on Ekiti State and its different towns in general, but its festivals, most especially the Egbegun Festival has so far been treated as unimportant. This work tends to address the importance of the Egbegun Festival and its roles in the political economy of Yorubaland. Its findings would add to the already existing knowledge of cultural traditions and further enhance the significance of cultural festivals and their benefits to Yorubaland and Nigeria as a whole. It is the aim of this study to give a documentation of the Egbegun Festival given its historical heritage, its importance and significance in the political economy of Omuooke Ekiti community. It thus examines the Egbegun Festival of Omuooke Ekiti in the context of its overall contributions to the development of Yoruba culture and economy.

SCOPE OF THE STUDY

Omuooke Ekiti is a Yoruba community in Ekiti State spread over a large territory. The town is divided into three administrative districts: Isalu, Otun and Osi; each with its different quarters. The scope of this study covers the Omuooke community's Egbegun Festival from its historical origin to its present organization and celebration, with emphasis on the Festival's economic impact on the political structure of the community and Yorubaland.

LITERATURE REVIEW

This section is thus devoted to reviewing literature related to the study, as not much has been documented regarding the Egbegun Festival. The Yoruba hold a deep faith in the power of symbols and public presentations of festivals, to produce the desired effects for the betterment of the community. Fola Akinrinsola in his article on Ogun Festival in the Nigeria Magazine, June 1965, stated that; 'In Ondo, few traditional festivals of any importance survive to this day. The most important of these is the Ogun Festival which is celebrated with pomp and pageantry and with much gusto partly because devotees of the god believe he is the god of peaceful living and partly because the Christians and Muslims who participate actively in the festival see the celebration as a revival of a great traditional heritage.'[4]

Leslie Prosterman in his book, Ordinary Life, Festival Days: Aesthetics in the MidWestern County Fair, 1995, supported Akinrinsola's work when he state that 'traditional festivals, in many ways, are the past made present, which as historical constructs, may legitimate actions of the present.'[5]

This fact is true of the Egbegun Festival because during the festival, the consciousness of the Omuooke people's heritage comes alive and the significance of the festival lies in its contribution to the preservation of the age-long tradition of the Omuooke community. Moses Okeke in his article, 'Precepts for Tenure Ethics in Yoruba Egungun(Masquerade) Proverbs' published in the Journal of Pan-African Studies, posited that, the Egungun Festival is an annual re-affirmation or re-enactment of the social contract between the ancestors and the community which marks the institutionalization of periodic social commentary and communal appraisal of the community. Thus he said, 'the Egungun enjoy much reverence and adoration from the community in the same measure that people expect much from them.'6

Moses Okeke's work buttresses Bame Kwabena's work, Profiles in African Traditional Popular Culture: Consensus and Conflict, Dance, Drama, Festival and Funerals, where Bame stated that, Festivals as socio-cultural events, have also become for many communities a symbol for ethnic citizenship.7

The Egungun Festival of Yorubaland can be likened to the Egbegun Festival of Omuooke Ekiti which itself is a re-enactment of the social contract between the ancestors and the community. It affords the people the opportunity to relive memories of their ancestors in the past that have been passed down to them. And so, it is a highly cherished cultural festival among the Omuooke people. Furthermore, Ajayi I. O. in his book, Odun Egungun ni Ile kaaro-Oojiire stated that, Egungun ceremonies take place in order to honour ancestors. Offerings are made to ancestors and performances help to remind people of the lives of their ancestors, while helping to reinforce the relationship between the living and the dead.8

Oyefolu A. Taye, in his article on 'Cultural Festivals in Lagos State', opined that One thing of note is that the Eyo Festival of Lagos brings all the people under one umbrella and promotes oneness among the people.

The Festival has a complete paraphernalia which consists of white flowing gowns that cover the head and feet.9

This is also true of the Egbegun Festival because it unifies its members and enhances continued cooperation among surrounding communities. The Egbegun Festival also has a complete paraphernalia which consists of an all-white attire. As further explained by Oyefolu A. Taye in his article, the Ebibi-Agemo festival is one of the major socio-historic festival among the Ijebu, when people call on the deity for more blessing in all their human endeavours and also a period when the socio-economic activities of the town boom. According to him, the festival is always full of sight and sounds that give immense entertainment to all spectators, both indigenes and visitors. This is however not what is of real importance in the festival. He further stated that the artistic aspects-costumes, acrobatics, singing, drumming, dancing, community fellowship, and feasting-important as they are, are not the ultimate function of the festival or any other festival among the Yoruba. Thus, when attention is carefully paid to the underlying ideas of the festival, it becomes obvious that one ought to go deeper than the artistic surface if one hopes to reach and benefit from the social message that the festival strives to portray.10

Relating this to the Egbegun Festival, Oyefolu's article stands in line with Olaitan and Oladipo Idowu's work, Omuooke-Ekiti, Yesterday and Today, where they stressed the fact that 'the significance of the Egbegun Festival, lies not in its festival activities, but in the initiation and graduation of one age grade to another.'11

This gives insight into the fact that the Egbegun provides useful training for responsible citizenship in youths and adults in the town, involves youth initiation into adulthood and the beginning of mature participation of youths in the affairs of the Omuooke community. Going outside Yorubaland, Ulli Beier in his article on the Osezi Festival in Agbor, Nigeria Magazine, 1963, stated that, the Osezi Festival of Agbor is a festival that runs through a period of seven days with each day having a specific function. It is a brilliant spectacle, gay, colourful, but also intense and exhilarating. The Osezi Festival becomes a tremendous demonstration of loyalty on the part of the people of Agbor towards their king.12

The same can be said of the Egbegun Festival of Omuooke Ekiti. It runs through a period of seven days also with each day having a specific function. It is also a very colourful ceremony with brilliance and gaiety attached to it; and it is also the period when the Omuooke community-chiefs and the people renew their allegiance and loyalty to the Olomuooke of Omuooke in his palace. Likewise, T. N. Tamuno in his article on Odum Festival in the Nigeria Magazine, 1968, posited that 'the Odum festival of the Ijo clan is a rare event; hence, the excitement associated with it is not ruined by short-term cyclical performances. He further stressed that traditionally, the Odum Festival marked both a religious and social event. It was an act of worship of nature spirits as well as providing entertainment by demonstrating an art of high esteem among seafarers.'13

Oyin Ogunba supports Tamuno's work, in his article on 'Ceremonies', published in S. O. Biobaku's edited work Sources of Yoruba History, where he stated that, Festival rites are important for several reasons: first, they are the chief media of the religious expression of the people; Secondly, the institution of the festival is in itself a giant cultural establishment which can accommodate virtually every experience of the community and mould it into its own special idiom.14

In practice, therefore, the Egbegun Festival often achieves more than mere religious expressions and has material that can be an important source for the reconstruction of Yoruba history once the idiom is understood. A. Fajana in his article on 'Age Group in Yoruba Traditional Society', published in the Nigeria Magazine, 1968, opined that 'the age-group as an institution was, in the first instance, a convenient means of differentiating 'seniors' from 'juniors' in a society where seniority was of a great social importance.

Among the Yoruba, he said, it was usual to show respect to those older than oneself. This meant that a senior age-group had the right to direct and command a junior one if necessary. In this way the institution provided a suitable means by which public duties could be performed according to accepted principles. He went on to stress that training in physical fitness was particularly necessary because strength and agility were required at almost every stage of development. The age-group was the guardian of public morality and each was a censor morum for its own members.15

Now, A. Fajana's article corresponds with the structural organization of the Egbegun which involves age-groups from the least to the most senior. The Egbegun structure has the Iyoyo as the least age-group, followed by the Owoyin, then the Andare who graduate on the day of the Egbegun Festival. The Festival itself cuts across the social status of three senior age grades that must have been initiated on their graduation day. Buttressing this, Oyin Ogunba stated that, the structure of a Yoruba Festival is such that as one goes through the ceremonies of a typical Yoruba community, it is as if one is going through time itself with the dark past suddenly being illuminated and the present, teeming with life.16

And one such festival is the Egbegun festival of Omuooke Ekiti.

SOURCES AND METHODOLOGY

This study will adopt a detailed descriptive and analytical approach of historical presentation. Emphasis will be laid on the significant role festivals play in the political economy of Yorubaland, using the Egbegun Festival of Omuooke Ekiti to weigh the importance of cultural and traditional festivals in the society. The Sources are basically primary evidence and these include data extracted from oral history, chief of which is interview. Knowledgeable resource persons, chiefs, elders and community leaders, the King himself and persons of substance in Omuooke Ekiti were interviewed. In addition, some data were derived from library research especially that of the Institute of African Studies. The work is organized in chapters and sub-themes.

CHAPTER TWO

EARLY HISTORY OF OMUOOKE EKITI

The town presently called Omuooke Ekiti was founded many centuries ago by a strong and powerful legend called Olumoya. The name given to the town by Olumoya was Omuwo, a commercial centre and a linkage town between the Yoruba in the North such as the Yagbas, Ijumus, Kabba (the Owes) the Bunus, lokoja (Kogi), Ilorin, Bida (Nupes) and the Yoruba in the West such as Ekiti, Ijesha and the Oyo. Omuooke Ekiti at present shares common boundaries with Idofinaye now called Iyamoye, Eriti, Bolorunduro now a part of Kota, Araromi-Oke and Igbagun. She is about 500 kilometres above sea level and is situated on fairly plain land. Omuooke enjoys sufficiently annual rainfall brought about by Southern Westerly winds, the so called rain-bearing wind. During the month of November to February, the North-east dry wind from the Sahara dominates and brings in the dry season. The rainy season starts from March and ends in October or November. The vegetation is deciduous and the flow of many streams, ponds and rivers in the area is mainly seasonal during the rainy season. There are six streams in Omuooke Ekiti which drain the town. These are Amote, Amoye, Ayo, Odogbo, Ogbogun and Esiko. Amoye and Esiko serve as the main sources of drinking water, while other streams served early inhabitants of the town for their domestic purposes like building, bathing, washing and cooking. It is instructive to know that most settlements originated and thrived near rivers or on river banks and confluences.

The inhabitants of Omuooke Ekiti speak a common sub dialect of the Ekiti-Yoruba language and claim a common historical ancestry with other Ekiti people in particular and the Yoruba in general. Omuooke Ekiti is a typical traditional African society without written documentation of her early history as other parts of Ekitiland. Historical facts about the land were handed down orally from generation to generation until education was extended to the Yoruba and specifically to Ekiti and Omuooke people and thus began to emerge some documentation of its history. Omuooke Ekiti people are law abiding, peaceful and accommodating. They love strangers and visitors as much as themselves and their neighbours. The people chiefly engage in farming; an average man is either a farmer, a trader, palmwine tapper, an artisan or professional. The soil is fertile and supports the growth of food crops; like yam, maize, cocoyam, cassava and cash crops like coffee, kolanut, palm oil and rubber. The traditional governance of the town is structured hierarchically with the Oba as supreme head and other chiefs representing different sections or districts, quarters and clans.

The town maintains the concept of a universal deity because the people regard the numerous gods as intermediaries between them and the supreme deity. The town has long been associated with numerous norms and traditional festivals such as Egbegun, Itomo, and New Yam (Emidin). The community is further arranged into age grades and sets; each promoting peaceful co-existence and contributing in part for the survival of the whole. Marriages and commercial activities within and outside her immediate environment also contribute to harmony in the town. Omuooke Ekiti, just like other Yoruba towns, has been affected by both continuity and change; though it has preserved its traditional identity, certain inevitable changes have occurred in the process of development and modernization.1

ORIGIN, MIGRATION AND SETTLEMENT

 R. S. Smith in his work Kingdoms of Yoruba, has noted that there has been uncertainty as to which town can properly be considered as belonging to Ekiti in the late 19h century. All authorities seem to agree that the four leading rulers are: 'the Ore or Owore of Otun, the Ajero of Ijero, Ewi of Ado and Elekole of Ikole.'2
In Revolution and Power Politics in Yorubaland 1840-1893; Ibadan Expansion and the Rise of Ekiti Parapo, S. A. Akintoye stated that relying on the traditions of the Ekiti, the Ekiti country was made up of sixteen kingdoms.3
R. S. Smith has also shown that the following sixteen towns have been included in different lists: Efon Alaye, Ogotun, Iddo, Itaji, Ikere, Aiyede, Igbaraodo, Oye, Omuwo(which is now called Omuooke). Omuo, as presently claimed is a historical conglomeration of different independent towns each with its own ancestral origin. Such towns include: Ejurin, Ilisa, Ishaya, Igbeshi, Ahan, Iludofin, Oruju, Ijero, Iworo, Irafun, to mention a few, with each having its own ancestral leader. Ire, Ise, Isan, Aramoko, Okemesi, Emure and Akure have all claimed to derive their crowns and dynasties from Ife.4
The origin of Omuooke Ekiti like those of most towns in Ekiti and Yorubaland has been traced to Ile-Ife. Most towns in Yorubaland have no documentary evidence of their own origin, migration and settlement. They all relied on oral sources linking their origin with Ile-Ife. This situation is also true of Omuooke Ekiti as it is one of the problems of historical reconstruction. The existence of Omuooke Ekiti has been substantiated by her long periods of artefacts recorded. If a town really exists and cannot preserve its existence, then the existence is worthless and therefore narrates a pathetic story of a town trembling merely in darkness. The town has been able to preserve her true existence and her orally documented activities and this shows the superiority of their claims. The oral traditions on the origin, migration and settlement of Omuooke Ekiti are precise. The legend about the origin of the town is woven around Olumoya, the son of Odede

(Oranyan) who was regarded as the father of the town. The decision of Olumoya to leave Ife was as a result of the failure of both himself and his father to avenge a bad treatment meted on them. Before he left Ile-Ife, he consulted an Ifa oracle. The consultation gave him instructions stating that he was to permanently settle anyplace he observed three signs which were the footmarks of elephants, a thick forest and a lake. Olumoya on his journey reached the predicted place and saw a lake, he shouted: 'Omi O, meaning 'Oh Water'. From this proclamation, the name of the town Omuwo emerged. He moved a few distance from the lake and erected some houses where he settled with his followers. He called this settlement Ilemo after the name of his original home in Ife-Iremo. Today, the name Ilemo still exists till date in Omuooke. Olumoya, following the prediction of Ifa named other locations as follows:

(a) Odo-Igbo, meaning a lake in a thick forest, named after the lake he found.

(b) Erinjo, meaning elephants danced here, in the place where he saw the footmarks and trappings of elephants. These identities exist till date. To accord his new settlement Kingship identity and in recognition of his power and supremacy over his followers and other neighbouring villages, Olumoya acquired his own deities called Ipara era, a place recognised for the installation of powerful kings and this place is still recognised for such special ceremony till date. With this identification, Olumoya therefore became the first king of Omuwo and was recognised in his own kingdom as the Olomuwo of Omuwo. About eleven others succeeded him from generation to generation. With his conquest and those of his children, other villages that joined him still have their ancestral lands as farms which they call apole meaning initial settlement. They include: Ipere, Inigun, Ogege, Esa, Aroju, Abepe, Oyi, Odogbo Arufe, Areko, Elegbeta, Ekomo, Ijorun, Ogbagba, Igboolohun foho, Ododa, Ajasa, Abuta, Ikiwi, Okeigbo, Arosomi. Olumoya was succeeded by one of his children called Ogungbemi, who followed the good work of his father by expanding and re-organising the kingdom into three administrative districts which are: Isalu, Otun and Osi.

(i) Isalu is made up of five quarters namely: Akasa, Igbale, Ebiogidi, Ilebojo (Okesasa, Okelebojo, Odolebojo and Aragba) and Eemoba (Okeaofin and Odo atiba).

(ii) Otun consists of Odoejio, Erinjo, Odoelegun and Okeare/Idesunmoba.

(iii) Osi comprises: Arufe, Ilemo, Igbemisi and Okeringun. The structuring into administrative districts was based on the compatibility of the quarters and their closeness to their ancestral lands without much boundary disputes. Each quarter has a head who is a member of the district council and each district has a head that presides over the district council and becomes answerable to the king. The king also has assistants and advisers drawn from the districts. This structure allows for a representational, functional and peaceful administration of the town which is still followed till date. Other kings that followed such as Asakooko, Ipinlaye, Atere, Olukaka, Orisadamitan, Famokun, Alogunlowo, Adekunmi, Olupinla and Adebayo, all concentrated on the economic, social, political and infrastructural development of the town without tampering with the administrative structure as laid down by their forefathers. In other to expand the developmental and commercial activities of the town, the above mentioned Obas adopted peaceful diplomatic and non-conflicting relationships with other surrounding towns for a harmonised commercial existence. These towns include Ejurin, Ilisa, Igbede, Irafun, Ishaya, now called Kota. With further development, other towns registered their membership of the group, so that they could participate fully in the commercial activities affecting their respective communities which was strengthened by the presence of the British businessmen and administrators, who were directly in charge of the area. Such towns that became business members of the group include: Iludofin, Oda, Ouju, Ilisaodo, Ijero, Iworo, Igbesi (Ayebode) and Ahan. Each of these towns had its own traditional practice and Oba before participating in the business activities of the group, whose headquarter was at Omuooke. The group became very unwieldy for the convenient administration of the colonial masters because of their lack of compatibility in certain respects and they were not close together in settlement.

This situation made the colonial masters develop an administrative strategy where they divided the group into two for administrative and business convenience under the existing names Omuwooke and Omuwoodo. Omuwooke was made to stand on her own, while other towns that came purposely for business linkage decided to form a group called Omuwo Odo to enable them develop on their own, their business and political interests. These independent towns include: Ejurin, Irafun, Ilisaoke, Isaya, Igbede, Iludofin, Iworo, Oda, Oruju, Ijero, Igbesi(Ayebode) and Ahan. These towns came together based on certain criteria such as compatibility in ideas, culture, common dialect, similar level of commercial development and geographical nearness. The need for them to have a powerful leader that could join them together politically and be of great challenge to Olumoya's descendants at Omuwooke resulted into their having a contemporary king called Olomuwoodo of Omuwoodo, now known as Olomuo of Omuo. A name that arose through a long period of dialogue among members as regards the development of language and civilisation.

The Olomuwooke changed to Olomuooke of Omuooke that is the supreme leader of the people of Omuooke town. To create an unequal relationship between the two names, Odo was removed to read Olomuo of Omuo, giving the impression that Omuo is superior to Omuooke. It is difficult to have Oke (up) of a pair without Odo(down) when it comes to tradition and settlement; a situation that is difficult to believe in Yoruba contemporary history and settlement. These independent towns retained Olomuo of Omuo as their supreme king and Omuo as their town, while their ancestral towns became subsidiaries (quarters) of Omuo and their ancestral kings or Obas were reduced to chiefs, under the rulership of Olomuo of Omuo.

With this arrangement, these independent towns gave up their ancestral kingship in favour of the Olomuo of Omuo, their paramount ruler and symbol of unity, in response to challenges posed by the Omuooke community and the recognition accorded the Olomuooke of Omuooke traditional rulership and business supremacy in the early colonial era. These members of the group still retained this arrangement till date that is, the earliest towns like: Iludofin, Ilisa, Ijero, Iworo, Oruju, Ilisa odo, Ilisa oke, Irafun, Isaya, Ejurin, Igbede, Igbesi(Ayebode) and Ahan have chiefs instead of kings or Obas as it existed with their ancestral towns or villages many centuries ago. Omuooke retained her identity and therefore is never referred to as a subsidiary of any union.5

EGBEGUN FESTIVAL IN HISTORICAL PERSPECTIVE

According to Professor S. O. Olaitan in an interview in his residence, the Egbegun Festival is celebrated in remembrance of the organised war efforts of the founders of Omuooke. These founders originated from Ilemo in Ife several years ago through Olumoya, one of the sons of Oduduwa. Olumoya was directed to move out from his father's compound and travel towards the North for settlement, as directed by Ifa Oracle. On his journey he fought series of wars but since he was guided by the oracle, he was never defeated because of his obedience.

The land in which he settled was not his own but he had to fight series of wars to conquer the settlers before he could own the land. On his settlement, he had to annex those he conquered and ruled over them. He became friendly with them and organised them into clans according to the dictates of Ifa. He also engaged in training and retraining many of them into warriors for more conquest and expansion; he then moved out several kilometres to own land and people as directed by Ifa Oracle. He continued, stating that for every hamlet or group of people conquered, Olumoya established his rule and took with him some of the energetic able bodied persons away as slaves. He used these slaves for farming and all other domestic activities while he married off the women to his kindred in order to have a large army which he used for more fighting and conquest.

During slave trade, most of the children of the conquered people were sold into slavery and after his death as a king and warrior, his successors that is his own son, who had been groomed and empowered spiritually to continue with his father's conquest. This act continued until the several wars between Oduduwa's children in the south and those of Usman dan fodio from the north, which were tagged as the 'war of all wars'. But Omuooke could not be defeated until Lord Lugard came into the war with canons, guns and gunpowder and settled at Lokoja, about a hundred kilometres from Omuooke and this stopped the wars between Oduduwa's and Usman dan fodio's children. The memory of this organised warfare lingers on and gave rise to a social ceremony of war effort known as the Egbegun Festival today. The meaning of which is the consciousness and remembrance of the people as regards the organised warfare of the founding fathers of the Omuooke community.6

SIGNIFICANCE OF THE EGBEGUN FESTIVAL

The significance of the Egbegun Festival to Omuooke Ekiti cannot be overemphasized. It is a historic event in Omuooke community and as such, it is one of the most cherished and highly valued festivals in the town. The Egbegun festival contributes to the preservation of the age long oral tradition of Omuooke people. It provides an avenue for the town to make more friends with other communities around and boosts the economic development of the community. Also significant is the fact that it provides an opportunity for Omuooke sons and daughters who reside outside the town to come home and contribute their own quota to the development of the community.

The Egbegun Festival raises to a high esteem the social outlook of the Omuooke community. In an interview with Professor S. O. Olaitan, he stated that, the festival is a very important social ceremony in the community because firstly, it keeps on the memory of organised war efforts of the Omuooke founding fathers. Secondly, it helps to organise the youths into social combat groups for the defense of the community.

This is significant because it affords useful training for responsible citizenship in youth and adults in the town, as it trains the youth in combat readiness to defend the town in case of any outside aggression or attack. Thirdly, the Egbegun festival is important to the Omuooke community because it helps to increase bravery and self-sacrifice among the youths of different grades in the community.7

As much as the Egbegun festival prepares and organises the youth into combat ready groups, it also helps train the community members to become more vigilant in providing security for the community both day and night. A major significance of the Egbegun festival worthy of note is that, it enables the community members give continued respect to the kinship and other Chieftaincy titles, as the stability of the political structure determines how well the festival would go. The Egbegun festival equally affords the people of Omuooke the opportunity of worshipping their deities and passing over the ritual from generation to generation.

CHAPTER THREE

CULTURAL FESTIVALS IN YORUBALAND

An important determinant of human behavior and societal change in social system is culture. Culture is acquired through socialization, which is heavily influenced by the value system of a social group within the context of the social set up. Culture is viewed as a set of historically created decisions for living explicit or implicit, rational or irrational lives, accumulated overtime and transmitted from generation to generation as a necessary guide for human behavior, either through writing or practice.1

Festivals reveal the culture of every society in the world and they are specially performed. A festival is a means of re-emphasizing and uplifting one's culture to the advantage of recognition, spell casting and maintenance of balance in the society.2

Oyefolu A. Taye, in his view, opined that the main purpose of cultural festivals in Yorubaland is to protect and preserve the existence of the Yoruba heritage. These cultural festivals showcase things that will promote growth and integration among the Yoruba, including those outside Nigeria. There are many weekly, monthly and annual festivals in traditional and contemporary Yoruba societies in Nigeria. According to him Christians have two major holidays-Easter and Christmas. In the same vein, Muslims have two major holidays-Id El Fitri and Id El Kabir. On the other hand, traditionalists are petitioning for their own holidays and organise festivals to celebrate all traditional religions and the birthday of Orunmila, one of the Yoruba deities. Some community festivals cut across all religions such as Ojude Oba which is celebrated on the third day of Id El Kabir by Ijebus of all religions and focuses on paying homage to the traditional king of Ijebu Ode, the Awujale.3

Some of the better known festivals in Yorubaland are Oke badan and Osun Osogbo festivals. Others include: Egungun festival, Eyo festival, Ogun festival, Oloku festival, Ifa festival, Oduduwa festival, Igogo festival, Oluorogbo festival, Gelede festival, Orisa nla festival, Sango festival and Oba festival, to mention but a few.

STRUCTURE OF THE EGBEGUN

As the name implies Egbe Ogun meaning war age group, is the traditional way of training people to defend the town and co-operate with adults in the development of the town. Egbegun is symbolic of a town with a military force to defend it and the kinship from outside invaders or threats. The Egbegun is structured into groups which are: Iyoyo, Owoyin, Andare, Egbemeta and the Agba called adults.4

Youth Stages Egbemeta and Adult Stages . Andare .Owoyin . Iyoyo Oriberan Kemogbe Kemoga Kemote Kejido Kewayin Keleko Kemeyo .

IYOYO

The Iyoyo is an age grade made up of young boys with a minimum age of 15years. These boys are cared for and nurtured by their parents as hopeful members of a useful group for the community in future. Ordinarily, they do not perform any function for the community as a group but they are obliged to dutifully serve their parents until they are fully ready for initiation into the Owoyin grade in future. The members of this age group are allowed by their parents to observe activities of other groups but are refused the right to participate in them until they are fully matured to get into the more senior age group.

OWOYIN

After a period of 7-9years, members of the Iyoyo graduate into the more senior Owoyin age group on the day of the Egbegun Festival. The Owoyin basically are 'recruits' ready to champion small errands and activities for the town till the next Egbegun Festival.5

They start first as a small group waiting for other Iyoyo members to make up their minds whether or not to join. Before the arrival of the next Egbegun festival, the Owoyin would have expanded into a recognizable group. The Owoyin age grade is recognised by the town for effective participation in community development activities at a low level. They are involved in payment of small levies, keeping the town clean, decorating public places for occasions, participating in the security of the town such as serving in the vigilante group, running errands for the King and the Palace Chiefs in terms of sending messages to community members through town criers and keeping the local streams and springs clean for use. They equally keep public places like the palace, post office and town halls very clean. These assignments are based on their maturity at about a minimum age of 20years.

ANDARE

The Andare is an age group made up of individuals, newly graduated from the Owoyin. These are the actual 'military trainees'. Membership is voluntary because those qualified individuals who fail to enroll in the training throughout the period it lasts, will lose forever certain secrets of their forefathers during warfare and would be denied certain rights in that direction at adulthood, whether they are famous or not. For example, any individual who does not participate in the Andare military training cannot be installed as any of the following Palace Warrior Chiefs (Elegbe): Agbana, Olukosi, Olukotun, Oluju, Oosunla, Ogborin, Akogun, Elejofi, Elejoka. These Chiefs are recognised as Military Officers and still perform such functions as Palace Chiefs in the Oba's Council. Those who participated in the military training will not discuss issues and secrets relating to their training in a gathering where those who did not participate in the training are present. This practice still holds till date. The initiation into this group is secret and members are given the names of their forefathers at wars, which is different from that which they bear in public. This is necessary in case there is any invasion or shout for help during times of danger, so that names called or mentioned are strange names known only by the military members.6

During these 7-9years, there are midnight activities involved which are military in nature and happen every three months in a year. This always happens in the later part of the year.7

These midnight military activities take place at different secluded locations and the trainees are expected to fortify themselves to the training ground and to accompany themselves with certain apparatus which include palmwine to appease the gods who are expected to be in their midst during training.8

They equally carry searchlights known as opa made out of raffia leaves and about a hundred others. This searchlight is locally prepared and could withstand any rainfall or wind.9

At the end of the seventh or ninth year, the trainees are expected to graduate into the Egbemeta. The graduation itself is marked by a very colourful ceremony which brings people from all walks of life in Nigeria and the Diaspora to Omuooke to witness the ceremony.

EGBEMETA

The Egbemeta is a group of three (3). They are known as the Three Ranks and they hold the town. The Egbemeta of Omuooke Ekiti can be referred to as the 'Ministry of Defense' for the Omuooke community. They are titled Chiefs but perform the functions of Commanders under the Elegbe. If there is any trouble in the town, the Egbemeta has a duty to solve it and restore the community to its peaceful state.10

Their principal role is displayed at the Egbegun festival where they lead the new graduants and instruct them. The Egbegun festival cuts across the social life of three age grades that must have passed through the graduation process. On the day the festival begins, the most senior Egbemeta age grade bows out from the manual activities of the town and joins the Egbe Agba (group of elders); the second group next in line moves to the position where the most senior group has left and they become the new leading group of the Egbemeta, with their head Ata becoming the new Olori Egbemeta (leader of the group of three). The last group becomes the penultimate while the newly initiated graduants become the last age grade and these three age groups constitute the Egbemeta.

QUALIFICATIONS AND MODE OF SUCCESSION

There is no specific yardstick for the qualifications of the different age grades as it is quite simple. The first rule states that two friends or age mates from different parents would naturally be in the same age group because they share the same age bracket. Two brothers from the same parents cannot be in the same age group at the same time. The younger one would give way for the older one naturally. For instance, if the older brother is in the Andare, the younger one would be in that of the Owoyin. No two persons from the same mother can be in the same age group because it involves seniority. The elder one goes first, and then the younger one follows, then the third till the last male. Two half-brothers from either a different father or a different mother can both be in the same age group at the same time regardless of their age difference. A set of twins from the same parents can both be in the same age group at the same time because they are both of the same age. The only setback in this process is if one's younger brother passes through one age group before the older brother. If such happens, then the older brother misses his turn for life. It is irreversible. The simple basic rule for qualification is, once the older male is there, the younger male waits for his turn which naturally would be in the next seven to nine years.11

The mode of succession varies but it is quite simple. For the three basic young age groups- Iyoyo, Owoyin and Andare, the mode of succession falls between the ranges of seven to nine years. They get seven years if they have behaved well and the community is satisfied with them. But it extends to nine years if they in any way offend the community or prove stubborn.

Firstly, the Iyoyo after the stipulated seven years or nine years if otherwise, graduate into the Owoyin. The same thing goes for the Owoyin as they graduate to become Andare.

The Andare on their part, graduate into the Egbemeta on the celebration of the Egbegun festival. The mode of succession for the Egbemeta is a bit different from the others. The Egbemeta is a group of three ranks and on the day of the Egbegun festival, the most senior group bows out after haven served the community for twenty seven (27) years. As they leave, the new graduants take their place as the third group while the former second and third groups become the new first and second groups. Each group serves in the Egbemeta for twenty seven (27) years and on each Egbegun festival, the groups move one step up the hierarchical ladder. The new group replaces the group leaving to become elders in the community. No one calls them for any community job and they are equally looked upon with new found respect by the community. In an interview with High Chief M. S. Akomolehin (Ainda of Omuooke Ekiti), he said 'it is a rotatory process that is very impartial as nobody is sidelined and everybody gets his turn.'12

EGBEGUN FESTIVAL CELEBRATION

The Egbegun festival is done with elaborate planning and oganisation. In Omuooke Ekiti, the Egbegun is celebrated within a period of seven days, each with its own event. The festival is very important to the Omuooke community and it brings cooperation among the people.13

According to High Chief Orisadamitan (Agbana of Omuooke Ekiti), in an interview conducted in his residence, after Christmas and Easter, the festival follows because it is the most significant festival in the town that upholds the age long culture and tradition of the Omuooke people.14

In the same vein, Chief Olorunsogbon Benjamin, in an interview conducted in his residence, stated that, before the celebration of the festival, the leaders of the Egbemeta make preparations and plan for the success of the festival either by making sacrifices or anything of the sort. The Olori Egbemeta (head of the three ranks) informs the new group graduating before-hand on what to do and what not to do and if any information is to be relayed to the Kabiyesi before the festival, it would be done.15

On the eve of the festival, the group graduating, to fulfil traditional rites, would carry the opa (light made with bamboo leaves and raffia palms) which would serve as a torch, proceed to a particular point in the town, drop their light torches and leave it to burn out. On the festival day itself, each graduant would be clothed in a complete white attire (white cap, white singlet or t-shirt, white shorts and most importantly, a white shawl wrapped around the graduant called ala). They all proceed from a point called Idi Iroko, barefooted, silent and on a straight line along a mapped out path to a place called Ugbo Itomo (place where the initiation takes place). There a new leader is chosen as directed by Ifa Oracle, named by the Kabiyesi and the graduating group gets a new name which they would be known as for life. Each graduant holds onto whatever he believes in; it could be the Holy Bible or Quran, or a snail, salt, or anything one's head believes in.

Religion does not interfere with the tradition because it is the culture of the community. After the initiation, the new leader leads them out and they proceed to the market, a place called Atu. At the market, there is a shrine where only the new leader called Ata sees what is inside. This is followed by the certain incantations performed by the leaders of the Egbemeta and the chant goes thus:

Oriberan Ooo...(new graduants, now the third Egbemeta group)

Kewayin Ooo...(new second Egbemeta group)

Kemeyo Ooo...(new first Egbemeta Leaders) Then all the members that fall into these groups would chant in response:

Orise Oooo ... Oriponda ...

This is followed by the Elegbe's (Warrior Chiefs) chant:

Aiye abi Orun?(Is it earth or heaven)? Then the groups chant in response Orun ni Ooo ...(It is heaven).

The new head of the graduants then prays at the shine and leads his group to his house. There, he would pray for the entire group and ask for their support and backing. After all these activities, there would be merrymaking, eating, drinking, dancing and rejoicing. The Second day of the festival is the installation of new chiefs in the market. The new graduants would be given new titles such as Elesia, Olukotun, Olukosi, Sosoro and others.
Omuooke community is divided into three clans, the Elesia who is the overall second in command represents members from the Isalu clan and he becomes their clan head. The Olukotun represents members from the Otun clan and he also becomes their clan head. The same goes for the Olukosi who represents members from the Osi clan and equally becomes their clan head. But they all report to the Ata who is the general head of the group. For instance, the last Egbegun festival was celebrated in February 2010 and the group that graduated was named Egbe Oriberan. The leader is addressed as Ata Egbe Oriberan Omuooke Ekiti. The titles of others go thus:
Elesia Egbe Oriberan Omuooke Ekiti,
Olukotun Egbe Oriberan Omuooke Ekiti,
Olukosi Egbe Oriberan Omuooke Ekiti,
Sosoro Egbe Oriberan Omuooke Ekiti, to mention but a few.

After the titles have been given, the new chiefs go back to their families, friends and well-wishers dancing with joy and rejoicing. The Third day of the festival involves pledge making. The new graduants pledge their loyalty to the community's progress and peace to their Bale, one of the Amuru (Palace Chiefs) who would be their guardian. They dress in different attires that day. The Fourth day, the new graduants pledge their loyalty to their Ata and promise to stand by him always in all his decisions. On this day, the graduants all dress up wrapped with aso oke or gele as each graduant wants it. The Fifth day, the Ata and his group would dance round the Place called Atu in the market and proceed from there to the Olomuooke's Palace where on behalf of the new group, the Ata would pledge the service, loyalty and allegiance of his group to the Olomuooke, his Chiefs and all the people of the Omuooke Community. After that, the group goes back to their Ata's house and the merrymaking continues. The Sixth day involves personal visitation among group members and the community, and everybody congratulates each other. The merrymaking continues afterward. The Seventh day which is the last day is called Ije ceremony where the entire festival and all its activities from day one are celebrated. On that day, everybody moves to the New Palace arena, a popular musician is called to crown off the ceremony and everybody has a good time. Friends and well-wishers, including people from outside the country come to witness the occasion and celebrate with each other till dawn of the next day.16

S. O. Olaitan and Oladipo Idowu in their work, Omuooke Ekiti Yesterday and Today, stated that the essence of the Egbegun festival is the initiation of youth into adulthood marking the beginning of their mature participation in the affairs of Omuooke community after years of training in tolerance, endurance and bravery.17

The festival cuts across the social life of three age grades known as the Egbemeta and it is categorized thus: the first group is the Egbe Kinni, the second group, Egbe Keji and the third group becomes Egbe Keta. These three make up the Egbemeta also known as the 'Three Ranks'.

OFFICIALS OF THE EGBEGUN AND THEIR POLITICAL IMPORTANCE

In Yorubaland generally and elsewhere, traditional officials remain a very significant element in society which cannot be ignored. The officials of the Egbegun festival include:

Olomuooke of Omuooke (Paramount Ruler of Omuookeland)

Elegbe (Warrior Chiefs)

Egbemeta (Three Ranks)

These officials are those directly involved in the Egbegun festival and their political importance in the community is not overlooked. Chief Mrs. Mojisola Modana (Yeye Agidin of Omuooke Ekiti), in an interview, stated thus: they are the cultural leaders of the Egbegun whose political representation of the community is identified first before any other dignitary in the Egbegun celebration. Their importance is very significant to the Omuooke community because if any is absent from his duty post, the whole celebration is put on hold. And as such their presence is paramount to both the community and the success of the Egbegun festival.18

These officials head the whole programme. According to one Baba Pius Oladele Ogunleye, in an interview conducted in his residence, 'the Elegbe, headed by the Agbana, are in charge of the festival and they decide whether or not the candidates are ready for graduation. As it is, the Kabiyesi does not control what goes on during the festival; his only function is to name the new leader of the group after consultation, while the Egbemeta leads and instructs the new graduants on their new role as part of the Egbemeta. In essence, the Egbegun officials are the pillars of the festival and without them, there would be no festival at all.'19

CHAPTER FOUR

ECONOMIC IMPACT OF THE EGBEGUN FESTIVAL

Festivals and cultural events are the important drivers of tourism activity in Yorubaland. The Egbegun festival of Omuooke Ekiti, since its inception, has been a celebration of cultural traditional arts which has its exceptional features. P. T. Long and R. R. Perdue, in their view stated that, Festivals are organized for a variety of reasons. Some of these reasons include: enhancing or preserving local culture and history, providing local recreation and leisure opportunities, and enhancing the local tourism industry.1

The Egbegun festival has been a celebration of Omuooke cultural tradition. Attendees, both indigenes and visitors enjoy every aspect of the festival, the performing arts, music and dance representing the community's cultural tradition and that of Yorubaland. The festival attendees are offered the opportunity to take souvenirs of the festival away with them; that is, authentic traditionally made crafts, stickers, key-holders, almanacs, festival shirts with imprints of the celebration on them, face caps, to mention but a few. The festival experience is also enhanced by a variety of ethnic food types, both from the community and neighbouring communities who stand to gain economically from the festival, fostering more cooperation among them.

In an interview conducted with Chief J. B. Adewunmi (Elenta of Omuooke Ekiti), in his residence, he put forward that 'the impact of the festival on the Omuooke community occurs through spurring economic activity where there is increase in the price of foodstuffs and market produce solely due to the ceremony. It also occurs through expanding the cultural and artistic opportunities available to the Omuooke residents and it equally occurs through increasing the visibility of Omuooke Ekiti as a tourist destination. One significant role of the Egbegun festival is that it attracts more money to the local economy of Omuooke and increases tourist visits to the area. During the festival, visitors no doubt spend more money on food, hotel accommodation and transport services.'2

For exclusive festival visitors such as traditional rulers and chiefs, political officials, the media and visitors from outside the country, their highest expenditures are on lodging and accommodations. Local business owners who sell in retail categories capture the increased market by making goods available to the added consumers. And in doing this, these local business owners could provide more information to the festival visitors to promote local services, stores and restaurants.

The Egbegun festival further creates job opportunities for the community. Visitors and attendees would need guides, transport services and all the help they could get and these help provide more jobs for the community while the festival lasts. Owing to the fact that the Omuooke people are very friendly, their good natured friendliness towards visitors may encourage visitors to extend the length of their stay in the area and help increase the economic impact of the Egbegun ceremony. The festival officials could also encourage return visits by first time visitors and increase new visits by promoting the festival outside their community using the media of the visitors, their travelling sons and daughters and the neighbouring communities.

All of these actions raise the social status of the Omuooke community and further increases reverence for their indigenous political structure headed by the Olomuooke of Omuooke. It also better enhances the socio-economic cooperation between Omuooke Ekiti and other Yoruba communities on the one hand, and on the other, between Omuooke community and its surrounding neighbouring communities. In the Nigerian situation where press freedom is extensive, the coverage of traditional events such as the Egbegun festival, not only keeps the public informed but highlights local initiatives where the festival performances provide the driving force. This proves culturally that Nigerians hold a deep faith in the power of symbols and public presentations to produce the desired effects for the betterment of self and community.

POLITICAL ECONOMY OF THE EGBEGUN FESTIVAL

The Olomuooke of Omuookeland, HRH Oba Valentine Otitoju Adebayo, in an interview conducted in his residential Palace, opined that 'the indigenous political structure of the Omuooke community has always played a pivotal role in mobilizing the community for development. In the absence of a recognised political structure within any community, local government administration often becomes difficult.'3

In colonial times, even colonial administrators saw the importance of traditional rulers and used them for easy governance. Today, the role of the indigenous political institutions is even more important, such that it has been given a place of prominence in the national political and administrative systems. HRH Oba Valentine further stated that, 'politically, festivals afford the indigenous political hierarchy the opportunity to reassert their authority over their subjects and local citizenry.'4

And here lies the political economy of the festival. During the Egbegun festival, all subjects of the Olomuooke renew their allegiance and loyalty to the paramount ruler, the Olomuooke of Omuooke, by paying homage in the Palace. The Kabiyesi also gets the opportunity to reassert his authority over his subjects and people. The Olomuooke, his Chiefs and Elders also use the occasion to discuss political issues affecting the welfare of the Omuooke community. It unites the community and brings about cooperation. Petty disputes between the Kabiyesi and any of his Chiefs or among his Chiefs themselves are expected to be resolved. Equally important is the fact that the festival portrays the rich cultural heritage of the people, for all those who ensure that the Egbegun festival continues in its trend.5

This is illustrated by the traditional rites of initiation performed during the festival, the all-white attire of the graduants, the dances, drumming, songs, attire of the Egbemeta and that of the Elegbe, the blue-painted bodies of the new Andare and the Kabiyesi's regalia, all of which form important aspects of the festival. The political economy of the Egbegun festival shows most importantly that the traditional ruler is still the embodiment and custodian of Omuooke political culture and tradition and this generally applies to most Yorubaland. In the same way, traditional festivals show that the traditional rulers, kings and chiefs alike represent the embodiment and serve as custodians of Yoruba political culture and tradition. Festivals in Yorubaland are seasonal, colourful and elaborate ceremonies involving entire communities that rely on traditional values to sustain the people's interests. These ceremonies provide an opportunity for diverse groups to acknowledge the blessings of the 'Supreme Creator' and the lesser deities and ancestral spirits, manifested in good health, good harvest, abundance of children and the likes.

CHAPTER FIVE

SUMMARY/ CONCLUSION

The Egbegun festival of Omuooke Ekiti is a colourful public event that often expresses, reflects and reinforces community social relationships and cultural values. It is a celebration that not only relives the memories of the past, but also marks a significant event among the people of Omuooke community, whose ideas, aspirations and philosophy are transmitted for the purpose of social continuity.

The festival plays a major role in documenting the history and culture of the Omuooke people and the whole of Yorubaland. One of the festival's roles includes bridging the gap between the living and the dead which is well represented in ancestral worship and the passing of historical knowledge of the ancestors to the present generation. The festival's significance to the community cannot be over-emphasized. It raises to a high esteem the social status or outlook of the community and provides an avenue for the town to enhance cooperation and make more friends with the surrounding communities. In boosting the economy of the community, the Egbegun festival brings to the forefront the importance of the indigenous political institution, headed by the paramount ruler, the Olomuooke of Omuooke.

The political economy of the festival draws on the prominence attached to the indigenous political structures. It affords the political hierarchy the opportunity to reassert their authority over the subjects and unifies the people and their leaders as one. No doubt, the Egbegun festival is a prominent ceremony, full of gaiety with an aesthetic appeal and entertaining value that fosters oneness and unity among the people of Omuooke Ekiti.

CONCLUSION

For the people of Omuooke Ekiti, after the seasons of Christmas and Easter, the Egbegun festival is the next season in importance. The festival means everything to them. In the course of oral interviews conducted, everybody questioned gave the impression that the Egbegun festival is not just a festival or among the many festivals of the town, but it is 'the festival' that gives the community recognition and singles them out from other Yoruba communities because of the unique nature of the festival. It does not end there because within the Omuooke people, is an existing consciousness; a consciousness that involves reliving the memories of their forefathers.

Today, the initiation and graduation process of the Egbegun remains the same as it was laid down by their fathers. One principal observation during fieldwork was that whenever the Egbegun was mentioned, the people showed so much interest and excitement. But this was mixed with caution as the people feared revealing their culture and tradition to just anybody.

Religion does not affect, in any way, the Egbegun initiation ceremony even though some individuals are against its traditional hold on the Omuooke people.

The Egbegun festival, today, has a great hold on the Omuooke community and is one of the most significant and important festivals in the whole of Yorubaland. In spite of westernization and modernity, the Egbegun cultural festival is given prominent attention by the people of Omuooke Ekiti. This, however, is not a surprise because culture is highly valued by the Yoruba. It is their identity, their memory, their pride, their achievement and their contribution to world civilization.

BIBLIOGRAPHY

A. Primary sources
- Oral Interviews

B. Secondary sources
- Books
- Journals
- Magazines
- Articles

Books

. Ajayi i. O. Odun egungun ni ilekaaro-oojiire translated version (Ibadan: All Gold Publishers), 2005.

. Akintoye S. A. Revolution and Power Politics in Yorubaland 1840-1893: Ibadan Expansion and the Rise of Ekiti Parapo (London: Longman Publishers), 1971.

. Bame Kwabena, Profiles in African Traditional Popular Culture: Consensus and Conflict, Dance, Drama, Festival and Funerals (New-York: clear type press inc), 1991.

. Olaitan S. O. and Oladipo Idowu, Omuooke Ekiti Yesterday and Today (Bauchi: League of Researchers in Nigeria Publishers), 2002.

. Prosterman Leslie, Ordinary Life, Festival Days: Aesthetics in the Midwestern County Fair (Washington Dc: Smithsonian Institution Press), 1995.

. Smith R. S. Kingdoms of the Yoruba (London: Methuen Publishers Limited), 1969. -

Journals

. Long P.T., Perdue R. R. 'The Economic Impact of Rural Festivals and Special Events: Assessing the Spatial Distribution of Expenditures' Journal of Travel Research, 28 (4), 1990.

. Okeke Moses, 'Precepts for Tenure Ethics in Yoruba Egungun (Masquerade) Proverbs' Journal of Pan-African Studies, Vol 1 (9), August 2007.

Magazines

. Akinrinsola Fola 'Ogun Festival' Nigeria Magazine, 85, June 1965.

. Beier Ulli 'Osezi Festival in Agbor' Nigeria Magazine, 78, September 1963.

. Fajana A. 'Age Group in Yoruba Traditional Society' Nigeria Magazine, 98, September/November 1968.

. Parratt J. K. 'An Approach to Ife Festivals' Nigeria Magazine, 100, April 1969.

. Tamuno t. N. 'Odum Festival' Nigeria Magazine, 97, June/August 1968.

Articles

. Ogunba Oyin 'Ceremonies' in S. O. Biobaku (Ed) Sources of Yoruba History (Oxford: Clarendon Press), 1973.
. Oyefolu A. Taye Cultural Festivals in Lagos State Cefolass: Centre for Lagos State Studies, Friday, 16 July 2010.